ICC T20 CRICKET WORLD CUP 2024

Written by: Arindam Sain

****

INDIA WON AGAINST PAKISTAN IN THE ICC T20 WORLD CUP 2024 ON 09.06.2024 AT NEW YORK !!!

*"The Indian team looked relaxed as
they started their campaign with a
convincing victory against IRELAND;
whereas, after having a shocking defeat
against the USA, the Pakistan team is
still in shock, one can UNDERSTAND.
In the city, where there
is the 'Statue of LIBERTY';
the India Vs Pakistan match*

was played at 'Nassau COUNTY'.
The outfield of the stadium at
New York was a bit SLOW;
Kohli got out at 4 only,
which was a big BLOW.
Only 13 runs got scored
by the Indian SKIPPER;
but, it was a good knock of 42
by the Indian WICKETKEEPER.
Except Rohit, Pant and Axar, all the
other batters went out in a single DIGIT;
both Naseem and Haris took 3 wickets
each and they surely deserve the CREDIT.
On 09.06.2024,
India may have
scored only 119;
but, they bowled well too,
as three Pakistani batters
each could only score 13.
Bumrah bowled a delivery
which was the best ONE;
it was the turning point of the match,
when Rizwan got bowled out at 31.
Hardik got 2 wickets whereas Bumrah
finished his superb spell at 3/14;
India won by 6 runs as Pakistan
was restricted at 113."- Arindam Sain

****

ICC T20 WORLD CUP 2024 - WRITTEN BY ARINDAM SAIN

INDIA WON BY 7 WICKETS AGAINST USA ON 12.06.2024 !!!

"From the very first
ball, the Mr. Arshdeep SINGH;
took 2 wickets in the first over
to roar and rule like the 'Lion KING'.
Near the boundary line,
Siraj took an excellent CATCH;
Nitish Kumar is the highest
scorer for the USA in this MATCH.
Arshdeep Singh alone took
4 wickets conceding only 9;
in New York, even the score of 110 is
competitive to cross the target LINE.
Saurabh Netravalkar sent back Virat
and Rohit back to the PAVILION;
when Ali Khan bowled out Rishabh,
India was struggling at 39/3
and the match was ON.
The fielding of the USA team
was not up to the mark, on
which they must improve UPON;
India won by 7 wickets on
12th June 2024, as alongwith
Dube, the 'SKY' scored half a TON."- Arindam Sain

****

INDIA WON BY 47 RUNS AGAINST AFGHANISTAN ON 20.06.2024 !!!

"The 'Hitman' is not in good FORM;
and unable to PERFORM.
Rashid Khan, as usual,
did some early DAMAGE;
Dube must be replaced by Rinku

ICC T20 WORLD CUP 2024 - WRITTEN BY ARINDAM SAIN

from the next match, at this STAGE.
Suryakumar never bothers
about the pitch REPORT;
but always expects a batter at the
other end to give him good SUPPORT.
Hardik gave a good
support by scoring 32;
to win the match,
Afghanistan had to score 182.
In the 2nd over, Gubaz's wicket FELL;
Zadran got hunted by Axar PATEL.
26 runs scored by AZMATULLAH;
and 19 runs scored by NAJIBULLAH.
Nabi looked dangerous, but, it
was a good fight back by KULDEEP;
Jadeja took 3 catches, as if the ball was
just searching for Jadeja in the DEEP.
In the 47 runs victory against
Afghanistan, the Indian 'SKY'
has surely scored 53;
but, on 20.06 2024, at Barbados,
you also have to appreciate
and applaud Bumrah's 7/3."- Arindam Sain

****

INDIA DEFEATED BANGLADESH BY 50 RUNS ON 22.06.2024 !!!

"In Antigua, the place
is North SOUND;
the game was on at the
Sir Vivian Richards GROUND.
The 'Hitman' sang,
'I want to break FREE';
but, due to poor timing of a

shot, he could score only 23.

ICC T20 WORLD CUP 2024 - WRITTEN BY ARINDAM SAIN

Rohit Sharma was sent back
to the pavilion by SHAKIB;
both Virat and Suryakumar were
hunted by Tanzim Hasan SAKIB.
The 'reverse sweep' shot is a weak
point of Rishabh, that he must FIX;
it looked as if he threw away his
wicket at his score of 36.
Dube understood that at this juncture,
a partnership is an ESSENCE;
Hardik, as usual, knows how to break
the opponent team's line of DEFENCE.
Not only Hardik scored half a TON;
but also took the wicket of LITTON.
Kuldeep took the
wicket of TANZID;
even sent back the
good batter, TOWHID.
India defended 196 by 50 runs on
22.06.2024, as Kuldeep did an
excellent job with his 3/19;
then Bumrah and Arshdeep wrapped it up,
surely, against Bangladesh, what a splendid
bowling performance it has BEEN."- Arindam Sain

****

INDIA WON BY 24 RUNS AGAINST AUSTRALIA ON 24.06.2024 !!!

"Tame him if you CAN;
because he is the 'HITMAN'.
On 24.06.2024, Virat Kohli
got out by scoring 0;
but, Rohit Sharma
emerged as a SUPERHERO.
Rohit scored the fastest
fifty of this ICC T20 World
Cup 2024 TOURNAMENT;
he surely missed a ton by 8 runs,
but, the way he batted, it was a
pure classic ENTERTAINMENT.
Warner was not expecting
such an OUTSWING;
Suryakumar did justice to that
good delivery by Arshdeep SINGH.
To dismiss Marsh, it was
Axar indeed who took
an outstanding CATCH;

ICC T20 WORLD CUP 2024 - WRITTEN BY ARINDAM SAIN

*not only of Marsh, the Mr. Kuldeep
also took the wicket of Maxwell and
that was the turning point of the MATCH.
Once again, Head was becoming
the headache for the Indian team,
but, Bumrah slowed down the PACE;
after Head's dismissal, slowly and
steadily, India defended 205 by 24
runs to win the 'Super 8' round RACE."- Arindam
Sain*

****

INDIA THRASHED ENGLAND BY 68 RUNS ON 27.06.2024 !!!

ICC T20 WORLD CUP 2024 - WRITTEN BY ARINDAM SAIN

*"Guyana is a beautiful nation in
between Venezuela and BRAZIL;
on 27.06.2024, Rohit led from the
front before being bowled out by ADIL.
Rohit scored half a ton
and Suryakumar got
out by scoring 47;
Hardik, Ravindra and Axar also*

contributed well, as a result, the
scoreboard stopped at 171/7.
The reverse sweep can sometimes
become a huge BLUNDER;
as Axar felt so lucky by seeing
the foolishness of BUTTER.
Bumrah went for the KILL;
to bowled out PHIL.
Jos could
only score 23;
Axar also hunted Jonny and
Moeen to end up at 3/23.
Sam and Chris were not
watching Kuldeep's HAND;
maybe, that's why, the line and
length, they failed to UNDERSTAND.
Kuldeep even bowled out HARRY;
Jofrah looked in so much HURRY.
Due to some late hitting by Archer,
England could cross 100 runs
and end up at 103;
India won the semi final match
by 68 runs and Kuldeep had the
best bowling figure of 19/3."- Arindam Sain

****

INDIA WON THE ICC T20 WORLD CUP ON 29.06.2024 BY WINNING AGAINST SOUTH AFRICA BY 7 RUNS !!!

"It was the clash of
two unbeaten TEAMS;
it was the final match,
not as easy as it SEEMS.

ICC T20 WORLD CUP 2024 - WRITTEN BY ARINDAM SAIN

19

Oh ! Hitman, don't throw
your wicket like a DICE;
in the final match on 29.06.2024
Keshav Maharaj strikes TWICE.
When India was struggling at 3/34;
Axar Patel came in, to ROAR.
Virat Kohli played the kingly
knock when it matters the MOST;
de Kock sent back Axar who was
reaching near half a ton ALMOST.
Out of India's 176;
Virat alone scored 76.
It is very hard to understand
Bumrah's bowling TRICKS;
Jaspreet broke through the defense
to bowled out Reeza HENDRICKS.
Arshdeep repeated the
same length and LINE;
and due to smart captaincy by Rohit,
the de Kock had to depart at 39.
Suddenly, the Klaasen of
South Africa changed the GEAR;
and in the Indian camp, there was
so much tension and FEAR.
Hardik silently hunted KLAASEN;
and Bumrah simply stunned JANSEN.
Only one dangerous batter
was at the crease and
that was MILLER;

ICC T20 WORLD CUP 2024 - WRITTEN BY ARINDAM SAIN

*but, what an outstanding acrobatic
and smart catch taken by
Suryakumar to end the THRILLER.
India won the ICC T20 World
Cup 2024 final match by
defending their score by 7;
Powerful performance by the entire Indian
team and even Rahul Dravid celebrated it*

*so much as India won it after 2007."- Arindam
Sain*

****

ICC T20 WORLD CUP 2024 - WRITTEN BY ARINDAM SAIN

THAT TEAM HAS WON, IN WHICH,
ALL THE PLAYERS HAD THE 'NERVE OF
STEEL' !!!

"The ICC T20 World
Cup of 2024 is OVER;
but for that great victory by the Indian
cricket team, there is still HANGOVER.
In the USA, the popularity of
Cricket is not so LESS;
few years down the line, the 'Cricket' will
beat 'Base Ball' in terms of BUSINESS.
In 2023, when India lost the T-50 World
Cup, the entire team felt so DISAPPOINTED;
that triggered the desire to become more

ICC T20 WORLD CUP 2024 - WRITTEN BY ARINDAM SAIN

desperate to achieve what they WANTED.
Just like Shami made a comeback, Hardik
also did it too, to silence all his CRITICS;
Rohit believed that to get success,
there is no shortcut or TRICKS.
One must appreciate that
even small things do
make a great IMPACT;
the jumping catch by Axar against Australia
and the catch by Suryakumar against South
Africa will always be remembered IN FACT.
'We will make a comeback and win', that
should be the mentality of a champion
team and they should always FEEL;
in 2007 and in 2024, in ICC T20 World Cup
final matches, that team has won, in which
all the players had the 'nerve of STEEL'."- Arindam
Sain

****

Congratulations to the Indian Cricket Team for lifting the ICC T20 Cricket World Cup of 2024 !!!

****

*** THE END***